The Fancy Schmancy Lifeguard

Buddy x

Bella x

For
Stephanie and Natalie

Copyright © 2022 by Gilda Boram

Published by Rainbowdrop Books, an imprint of Rainbowdrop Enterprises.
All enquiries should be directed to www.RainbowdropBooks.com

Illustrations by Julian Boram.

ISBN 978-1-7399252-7-7 (hardcover) • ISBN 978-1-7399252-8-4 (paperback) ISBN 978-1-7399252-9-1 (ebook)

Book design by the Virtual Paintbrush.

Written by Gilda Boram   Illustrated by Julian Boram

The Fancy Schmancy Lifeguard

The Adventures of Two Travelling Poodles
An (Almost) True Story

This is a cautionary tale for anyone
who dares to judge a teeny weeny toy
poodle, by its fluffy puffy fleece.

My name is Bella.

And this is the story of my best friend Buddy,
who has a very big secret ...

When we get to the beach, Buddy doesn't do normal stuff like the rest of us.

Like jumping on sandcastles ...

Or digging holes ...

Or just relaxing (like me).

No.

Buddy runs straight to the lookout tower.
And he watches, and he waits.

I just know he's thinking about swimming
far out to sea and surfing the big waves.

Some call him WILD and WILLFUL, and just plain WEIRD.

But they don't truly know him like I do.

I call him SMART and SPARKY, and wonderfully SPIRITED.

You see, my best friend Buddy wants to be ...

A LIFEGUARD!

When we hear the scream for help from the lady caught in a rip ...

Everyone stops still, nobody makes a move.

Except Buddy.

He's the first one into the jet ski, ready for the rescue mission!

"Let's go, guys!" he yells, gripping on tight.

"What's this?" says the lifeguard. "A teeny weeny toy poodle?" All the lifeguard team laughs.

"I know I'm small, but I'm brave," he says, and his voice cracks, just a little.

Of course, they don't understand him.

The thing is, he isn't the type of toy poodle to give up!
Early the next morning, he's back in our pool, practicing.

Diving so daringly ...

Swimming
so strongly ...

Balancing so brilliantly ...

Then one day soon after ... DISASTER!

"We have the most exciting news," our parents tell us.

"We're moving to LONDON!"

But for Buddy, this was NOT good news, not at all!

"How can I be a lifeguard there?" he asks them.

Of course, they didn't understand him.

For everyone knows (and this is a fact)
THERE'S NO BEACHES IN LONDON!

The next thing we know, we're living a very
different life, and poor Buddy just isn't himself.

I try everything to cheer him up.
I take him to see the Queen ...
But he doesn't seem to care!

I take him to the theatre to see a show ...
But he just falls asleep!

And I take him out for high tea ...
But he doesn't eat a thing!

And I just know my poor Buddy is still
dreaming of living the lifeguard life ...

Then one sunny day later, there's a knock at the door. It's our new neighbour, the gloriously glamorous Contessa Giulietta from Geneva, saying, "There's a carnival in the park, my darlings, let's go!"

She's carrying her twins, Coco and Chanel,
in their very own bag!

On the way there,
she's chatting about
how she never EVER lets them out, for fear
that something HORRIBLE may happen.

When we get to the carnival,
we push through the crowd

And we can't believe our eyes ...

There's a huge pond,
with its own sandy beach!

Lifeguard
Tryouts Today

When Buddy sees the sign, he's the first to stand in line.
But nobody pays him any attention.

"Look at that fluffy puffy toy poodle!"
someone shouts out from the crowd,
and then everyone is laughing.

"The name is Buddy. With a capital B for brave," he tells the lady with the clipboard.

Of course, she didn't understand him.

"What's this? A fancy schmancy toy poodle who wants to be a lifeguard?" She's laughing, and with the swing of her arm we were banished to ...

The DOGS ONLY pond!

Suddenly ...

The Contessa is screaming

"MY BABIES!"

"HELP, PLEASE ... they cannot SWIM!"
For her tiny twin pooches have
escaped their prison bag!

Everyone stops still,
nobody makes a move.

Except Buddy ...

And in one astonishing moment he's ...

Diving so daringly ...

Swimming
so strongly ...

Balancing so brilliantly ...

Nobody can believe what's happening ... just me!

"BRAVO!" squeals the Contessa, scooping up her darling dripping duo. "You rescued them!"

She's holding Buddy up high in the air. "This poodle is a LIFEGUARD!" she announces, and the whole crowd claps and cheers.

And I've never ever seen Buddy happier until ...

Now.

My best friend Buddy has his OWN lifeguard team.
Everyone is welcome.

No matter how teeny weeny,
fluffy puffy or fancy schmancy.

Fun Fact

"The poodle was developed as a water retriever, and the distinctive clipping of its heavy coat was initiated to increase the animal's efficiency in the water."
–ENCYCLOPEDIA BRITANNICA

Lightning Source UK Ltd.
Milton Keynes UK
UKHW050745220422
401856UK00002B/68